Honeybrain

Tahlia Caputo

Presentation by *BookLeaf Publishing*

Web: www.bookleafpub.com

E-mail: info@bookleafpub.com

ISBN: 9789358319460

First edition 2023

ACKNOWLEDGEMENT

I acknowledge First Nations people as the traditional Owners of the land, skies, stars and waters and their deep connection to Country, encompassing spirituality, culture, language, family, law and identity. I pay my respects to Elders, past, present and emerging, who are the knowledge-keepers, passing on culture and tradition so that it continues to be preserved, shared and cherished. I encourage us all to tread thoughtfully and respectfully as we occupy Country to live, learn and connect. Always Was, Always Will Be.

griefcase

I carry around this griefcase
heavy, filled to the brim
forever trying to keep it orderly
tucked away, fit the fragments in

bedazzle it, embroider it to make it look
presentable
hide that it is worn and wonky
fragile
indestructible

I sell off some of my wares
helps to make it lighter over time
then I rush to stash it quickly
in a closet, car boot, their bed, the very back of
my mind

should have known
there is no parting with this griefcase of mine
end up left to lug it, drag it
up and down the endless flights

I carry around this griefcase
as much a burden as a treasure to me
searching for a secondhand store to dump it at
wanting nothing in return but peace.

Act I: arcade cowboy

murky waters
mundane matches
small talk, no spark
ghosted in batches

then a simple question of a "go-to song"
piqued my interest
spoke my language
played along

delicate digital stitches slowly sewn
through the screen of a critic
by an arcade cowboy with that belt buckle
and a smile that could wound a cynic

fairy lights, loud sounds
a fire pit, several rounds
all in black, effortlessly cool
a toy trinket offered by a giddy fool

magnetism, drawn in close
talked for hours, everything closed
too nervous to lean in...
"text me when you get home"

the start of something exciting and unknown.

Act II: cutie

turns out
we didn't need an arcade for games
they were there
in the way
you pulled me close
called me that stupid name
knowing it was casually cruel to leave me
wanting

turns out
you're no sharp shooter
just a fucking kid
brandishing a smart mouth and a toy gun
poking at bruises with careless fingers
but ready to run and hide
when you're called to come home

turns out
all of the best intentions
all of the careful cradling cannot compensate
for a lost boy with a toy trinket
too entitled
too scared
to ever call it what it was.

return to sender

I left a little piece of me
tangled in your soft, white sheets
in that room
filled with fern and flame and false advertising

made myself feel small
creeping past your family like a badly kept
secret
that you'd indulged in and then swiped from
your mouth

up creaking stairs
into a space that felt too movie set staged
to truly be a safe place to land
"this never happens"
though you truly could have told me anything at
all
I'd have unpicked my seams for you just the
same

perhaps it is twisted within the fairy lights
that cast a dim shadow
over the face you didn't want me to see
the one that held all of your reservations
as you bruised my pale skin with the hungry
mouth

on the other

perhaps it is bundled
in some other nondescript lover's garments
the ones you casually helped to discard
as you breathlessly explore them
making a mockery of the sacred space
I thought was mine to covet a little longer

does your sister ask about me?
that weird girl
who always raced up the stairs to hide away for
you
because she didn't know how to introduce
herself
"hello, I'm..." a friend... a fuck... a fool?

"you're a once off kind of person"
except it is twice now
that you have buried in under my skin
and then torn your way out again
a once off
so easily discarded

just that little piece of me remains
and when you finally find it

I hope that it has stained.

best before

could it be that the people
we are drawn to
despite ourselves
to spite ourselves

the ones we love hardest
who break us into smithereens
serve a purpose other than a lesson, a loss?

are we merely floating on this rock
with humans who will test us
the expiry with the gentle ones
coming long before it should

but we go in to bat
bleeding hearts
weeping wounds
for the ones who don't
won't
love us back

like it's a game
we were always certain to lose.

he

he
delicately and dutifully
dusts debris from dark days
with damaged hands and dazzling smile
he
a dream
and I am done for.

anxious attachment

can't bear to delete your face from my gallery
can't stand to see it either
can't listen to Gretta Ray or 'Silk Chiffon'
without feeling
like a punch in the teeth would be sweeter.

teacher's pet

he reaches in
pushes past the tendrils, the tangles and thorns
grabs the good, the bright
amongst the chaos
of my dark
with clumsy hands
and open mind

keeps me tethered, leaves me giddy
a schoolgirl crush on the most handsome teacher
with charm
and heart
and wit
and that fucking smile

-

the ground came hard and fast
too soon
confused
fat lip
bloody nose
just a schoolgirl tripping over herself
for the most handsome teacher
who has his own life to live

please, mister
explain to me, in all your wisdom and
worldliness
how two hearts
with these gashes and bruises and gouges and
stitches
can synchronise like this
and it still not be good enough
to eclipse a schoolboy's crush
on a long gone girl from a lifetime ago

if not now
then when
simply a serendipitous schoolyard scuffle
now only hurt feelings and scraped knees
to prove it was ever anything more
than a stupid schoolgirl's wet dream.

paying respects

I return to our past conversations
like a ghost
cursed to haunt my own grave

pouring over the words you said
when your hyperfixation
lulled me into a false sense of security

I revoke your access to me
like I am equipped
with weighted, rusty padlock and tattered KEEP
OUT sign

but my headstone has long been vandalised
a posy of flowers lay wilted and crumpled
as dead and dry as your potential

you critiqued my writing
like a teacher who had the right
then used your own like a weapon

a string of simpleton musings
keeping me tethered
to a truth that never was

you shouldn't speak ill of the dead
not even to your therapist
especially when you never even came by

to pay your respects.

disconnect

why is it I am cursed to collect connections?
stacking them neatly
cradling them gently
tending to them with such affection

always made to feel as if
you held a space for me
blurry boundaries helped build the walls
that kept out the closeness that could've been

celebrated your victories
mourned and burned with you, too
all too tough, too deep, too challenging
when it's your turn to come through

care so deeply
bravely show it
you feel chastised
let me know it

build up, chip away
then tear it down in sections
only scattered remnants left
of these battered and bruised
(dis)connections.

sacrilege

I want to feel your arms encase me
like I am something sacred
and you are virtuous and devout

I want to hear my name leave your lips
the most beautiful sound I've ever heard
like some divine, Holy word

I want to trace my fingers down your spine
like following a path that is new and unknown
but has been waiting for me my whole life

I want to watch you wake slowly
greet the morning light with your warm soul
like a born-again heathen witnessing a miracle

reverent
to this new found faith

reaching out
to bask in your Godly glow.

inconsiderate

sorry isn't enough
when you're only sorry about the burden
of your own guilt
sitting heavy on your proud chest
late at night

when you're not sorry
for skilfully opening my sternum
and filling it with all of your misplaced feelings
intimately stitching
so that they were kept safe inside

until your want for convenience
a fast-tracked family
had you hastily ripping at my seams

taking

breaking

desecrating

my home intruded upon
with nothing to show for it
but mess and debris

from the sledgehammer you took
to tear it all down
her name carved lovingly into the handle

I hope your daughters
are wary of men like you
so that the treasured wounds your carry
like badges of honour
are never theirs to suffer for.

holding on

changed the cover image
of that album full of relics
from your goofy, smiling face
to a terse quote that reads
"invest in people you invest in you".

not quite ready to wipe the memories
the proof
may need the reminder not to reach out
with my small, covetable hands
to help nurse your cherished wounds.

if it's any consolation
to you and the part of me that still simmers
we're both stuck doing time
paying the price
for wrongdoings that we didn't commit.

only I'm still trying to decide
whether it's a compliment
of an insult
that I was a placeholder
for a woman whose hands weren't afraid

to let go of the fucking rope.

shed

fluid
phases
serpent tongue
shedded
layers
come undone

cascade
feelings
don't you run
writhing
bodies
become one

old self
new self
crack and heal
fangs for show
but the venom real

distance
tugging
longing
stop.
fear the fall before the drop

unsure
unknown
black and blue
who am I
in spite of you?

howling

you had hoped
I wouldn't howl
across your cavernous withdrawal
said
"it's not personal"
tried to fool me
as if my weak eyes
and wary heart
didn't know better.

left me with your stinging silence.
close friend got your tongue?

you'd used a pen
your favourite weapon
to write me
to draw me
into your story
a mystified muse
now you tear the pages out
with the same hands you'd held me with.

replaced
replaced
replaced

is all that howls through the valley of untruths
you told
tended to gently; your leaves and lies so lush and
green

but it's always just rotted roots and dried up
promises
underneath.

peachy

I have fallen from the tree
onto uneven ground
bruised
dirty
more lost than found

outside soft
seeping
encasing a tough stone
detached from what gave me life
left to fester alone

you consume
pressing needy fingers into flesh
dripping
juicy remnants
down your chin and chest

devoured
too much too fast
always haste and hurry
choke
on my core
that stone heart now yours to carry.

room 308

I took a chance and she took a flight
felt the tension dissipate just for a moment
once the long-awaited embrace melted down my
trepidation
to condensation
droplets rolling down the shower walls as we
explored each other's skin and bone
under the fall of warm water
and our hesitation

we played the roles so well
indulging in the fantasy of a future we'd never
see
just for a couple of days
and nights
and 600,000 heartbeats or so
a little taste of something so sweet
it couldn't help but cause my teeth and trust and
tenderness to decay

a handwritten note
and oversized jumper to swaddle me
as I sob in crumpled sheets
and she jets to 35,000 feet
back to plants and pups and familiarity

and I know that mine is forever altered
as I try to hold tight to promises that I can
already feel
breaking
under the weight of my adoration

long distance is hard
but what is harder
is closing the gap and opening your ribs
a meek offering to a deity who had feigned
starvation
got her fill and left your bones awash with prints
and cracks and whispers of love
littered on the third floor
to erode, exposed
because burial would have been too costly.

a week of discombobulation.
running on autopilot. clunky, slow, masked.
feeling like I'm underwater, forever surrounded
by the infinite, black mass of fatigue.
can't decipher one thought from another.
just a swarm of bees, of noise in my mind.
try to connect. Square girl in a round world.
connection and futility become one in the same.
push forward. achieve. pay the price.
drag this triggered inner child around.
she shakes and cries. stop. can't hide. have to
show up.
show up. show up. show up. show up.
smile. eye contact. converse. breathe. blink.
appropriate. normal. expectations.

a week of discombobulation.
a lifetime of being held hostage by my own
brain.
clunky. slow. masked. try to breathe.
the air is thick with reminders of my
shortcomings.
and the shame.
the shame. the shame. the shame. the shame.
grit. look down. lose speech. choke. stare.

weird. strange. problems.
it just keeps piling. compounding.

every glimmer of hope, every second of relief.
enveloped by dread, by hours of grief.
a flood above my head and fire beneath my feet.
never right, never wrong.
existing just to be perceived.

inside my head is a lonely place to be.
inside my head is the only place I'm free.
inside my head is tangled, twisted, ugly.
inside my head
is a life sentence of me.

www.ingramcontent.com/pod-product-compliance
Lightning Source LLC
La Vergne TN
LVHW021349200726

843509LV00014B/2744